P9-DWG-207

The
Solar System
and Beyond

Black Holes
and
Supernovas

by Joan Marie Galat

Consultant:
Dr. Ilia I. Roussev
Associate Astronomer
Institute for Astronomy
University of Hawaii at Manoa

CAPSTONE PRESS
a capstone imprint

Fact Finders are published by Capstone Press,
1710 Roe Crest Drive, North Mankato, Minnesota 56003.
www.capstonepub.com

 Books published by Capstone Press are manufactured with paper
containing at least 10 percent post-consumer waste.

Library of Congress Cataloging-in-Publication Data
Galat, Joan Marie, 1963–
  Black holes and supernovas / by Joan Marie Galat.
    p. cm.—(Fact finders. The solar system and beyond)
  Summary: "Describes supernovas and black holes, including what they are, how they form,
and how scientists research them"—Provided by publisher.
  Includes bibliographical references and index.
  ISBN 978-1-4296-6004-4 (lib. bdg.)
  ISBN 978-1-4296-7225-2 (pbk.)
  1. Black holes (Astronomy)—Juvenile literature. 2. Supernovae—Juvenile literature. I. Title.
  QB843.B55G35 2012
  523.8′4465—dc22   2011004238

Editorial Credits
Jennifer Besel, editor; Heidi Thompson, designer; Eric Manske, production specialist

Photo Credits
Capstone Press, 17, 19, 21; ESA: NASA, ESO and Danny LaCrue, 6–7, P. Barthel, 29, V. Beckmann
(NASA-GSFC), 23; Getty Images Inc.: Joe McNally, 25, Oliver Burston/Ikon Images, 13; NASA, ESA,
HEIC, and The Hubble Heritage Team (STScl/AURA), 3; NASA, ESA, HEIC, and The Hubble Heritage
Team (STScl/AURA), 14; NASA, ESA, J. Hester and A. Loll (Arizona State University), 15; NASA, ESA,
The Hubble Key Project Team and The High-Z Supernova Search Team, 5; NASA/CXC/CfA/R. Kraft
et al, cover, 1, 26; Photo Researchers, Inc: Jeremy Bishop, 11, Lionel Bret, 18; SOHO (ESA & NASA), 8

Artistic Effects
iStockphoto: Dar Yang Yan, Nickilford

The author dedicates this book to Ellery, with love.

Printed in the United States of America in Stevens Point, Wisconsin.
092011   006391R

Table of Contents

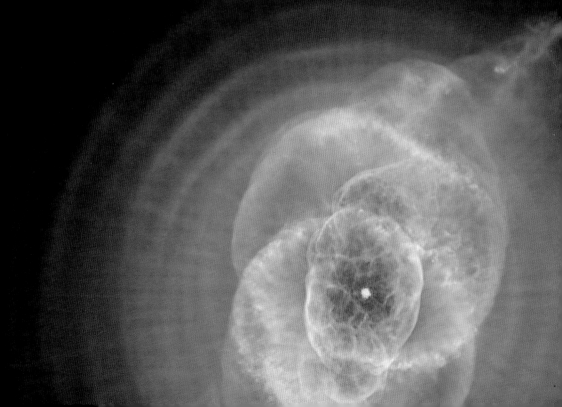

Chapter 1

Mysterious Events

The space far beyond Earth is full of mysteries. Through powerful space telescopes, astronomers have seen light that seems to bend for no reason. They've seen clouds of dust and gas that disappear. They see explosions that outshine entire **galaxies**. What's going on? It turns out that stars cause these amazing events.

Stars have life cycles, much like people. They are born and live for billions of years. When they grow old, some stars die amazing deaths. The largest stars go supernova, exploding gas and dust into the universe. Some supernovas lead to another mystery of space called black holes. Scientists believe black holes are the reason light bends strangely and clouds disappear.

The gas and dust that supernovas spread into the universe will eventually form new stars. Black holes pull in space matter, never to be seen again. These events are amazing pieces to the puzzle of the universe.

galaxy: a large group of stars and planets

a picture of a supernova in galaxy NGC 4526 taken by the Hubble Space Telescope

The Birth of a Star

Stars are born in clouds of gas and dust called **molecular clouds**. Inside the cloud, **gravity** draws gas and dust together into a spinning clump. The matter eventually begins to collapse in on itself and spin faster and faster.

The collapsing cloud creates huge amounts of heat and pressure. When it reaches a few million degrees, the core begins to burn. Heat and pressure make hydrogen atoms stick together and form helium. This process is called nuclear fusion.

During nuclear fusion, two forces work against each other. Gravity pulls dust and gas inward toward the core. Energy from burning hydrogen causes pressure that pushes outward. When the gravity and pressure become equal, the dust and gas stop moving inward. A star is born!

molecular cloud: a giant cloud made mostly of hydrogen atoms bound together

gravity: a force that pulls objects together

Tarantula Nebula, the largest known star-forming area

Star Sizes

All stars are gigantic compared to planets. But in the world of stars, some are big and some are small. Astronomers compare other stars to our Sun to get an understanding of sizes. Our Sun is about 870,000 miles (1.4 million kilometers) across. The smallest stars are half the Sun's mass or smaller. Mass is the amount of matter in an object. These small stars are low mass stars. A high mass star must be eight or more **solar masses**. All stars in the middle are called intermediate.

solar mass: the amount of matter in the Sun; one solar mass is equal to the mass of the Sun

Famous Stars

Star Name	Description	Solar Masses	Distance from Earth
Sun	closest star to Earth	1	93 million miles (150 million km)
Sirius	brightest star in Earth's night sky	2.3	8.6 light-years
Polaris (North Star)	visible year-round in the Northern Hemisphere, always pointing the way north	4.3	430 light-years
Proxima Centauri	closest star to the Sun	.1	4 light-years
R136a1	most massive star found to date	265	165,000 light-years

light-year: a unit used to measure distance in space; 1 light-year equals about 6 trillion miles (9.5 trillion km)

FACT: The largest star is thought to be 1,800 times bigger than the Sun.

Red Giants

After a few billion years, a star's core runs out of hydrogen. Then the excitement begins! Without fuel, nuclear fusion can't balance the pull of gravity. The outward pressure is gone. Gravity becomes the strongest force.

In a microsecond, the star's core collapses. Its temperature climbs higher than 100 billion degrees. The helium produces great amounts of energy. This energy causes the star to expand to an enormous size and turn red.

Small and intermediate mass stars become red giants. Over time, outer layers of red giants cool, expand, and blow away. The core shrinks into a chunk of carbon, forming a type of star called a white dwarf. After about another 10 billion years, the star completely runs out of energy. It becomes a black dwarf.

High mass stars form red supergiants. These huge, bright red stars have spectacular futures!

FACT: In about 6 billion years, our Sun will become a red giant and eventually form a white dwarf.

illustration of red giants
in a star cluster

Chapter 2

Kaboom!

Red supergiants are the largest stars. The cores of these stars have run out of hydrogen. They've started burning **elements** that collected in layers around their cores. Heavier elements such as carbon, silicon, calcium, and iron lay close to the core. Lighter elements such as hydrogen and helium gather nearer the surface.

A red supergiant burns its lightest elements first. When the helium is gone, watch out! The star begins to burn heavier elements for fuel. Eventually it can only turn silicon to iron. A star turning silicon to iron has only days to live. Iron can't fuse into something else and release heat. It also can't create enough pressure to balance gravity's pull.

element: a basic substance that cannot be split into simpler substances

Then gravity strikes again. It crushes the core into a dense ball. The core's temperature jumps to billions of degrees. It collapses so fast that giant shock waves blast the star's outer layers into space. This explosion is a supernova.

New Creations

Matter from a supernova floods the galaxy in an expanding cloud. This cloud is called a supernova remnant. Eventually the cloud's matter forms new stars. Supernova dust and gas formed the Sun.

During a supernova, atoms join together and create elements such as gold, silver, and uranium. In fact, elements on Earth came from a supernova. About 4 billion years ago, Earth formed from a dust cloud left by a supernova. The elements in the cloud became part of the soil. Today plants absorb the soil's elements. When you eat fruits and vegetables, you take the elements into your body. Almost all your body's elements came from stars! Supernovas created the calcium that's in your bones. They even made the gold or silver you wear.

Shock waves push away from a dying star during a supernova.

a supernova remnant called the Crab Nebula

The Remains

After a supernova, only the star's iron core remains. What happens next depends on the core's size. A core smaller than three solar masses crumples into a small **neutron star**. If the core is three solar masses or greater, gravity takes over again. The core collapses once more to create a black hole.

neutron star: a dark, spinning star with little mass

Chapter 3

Black Holes

The term black hole sounds like an empty place in space. It's really a place where gravity crams a lot of gas and dust into one spot. Imagine squashing a sponge into a small ball. The squashed sponge fills a smaller area. The same thing happens in space. Gravity squeezes a star's gas and dust into a spot smaller than an atom. That spot is a black hole.

Black holes contain more matter than any other object in the universe. They are also the densest objects. All their matter is crowded close together like the squashed sponge.

Forming a Black Hole

It takes less than a second for a black hole to form. Just after a supernova, gravity in the star's core crushes the star's leftover gas and dust. It squeezes all the matter into one spot called a singularity. The star is now a black hole.

The gravity in a black hole in incredibly strong. Stars, planets, or any space objects that get too near are pulled inside. Nothing, not even light, can escape. That's why it's called a black hole.

Black Hole Formation

Gravity

Heat

Gravity crushes the star's matter into an object called a black hole.

After a supernova, a high mass star can no longer create enough heat and pressure to balance gravity's pull.

Parts of a Black Hole

Scientists can't see black holes. But through research, they have a good idea of what one might look like. Picture a pointy cone with a gum ball at the bottom. The top of the cone is the event horizon. Like Earth's equator, this imaginary area describes a region in space. It marks where gravity becomes strong enough to pull matter inside.

The gum ball is the singularity. It pulls gas and dust into one tiny point. As more matter is pulled in, the singularity's mass increases. Gravity grows stronger, and the event horizon becomes larger. Only objects outside the event horizon's range are safe. They cannot be pulled into the hole.

artist illustration of a black hole

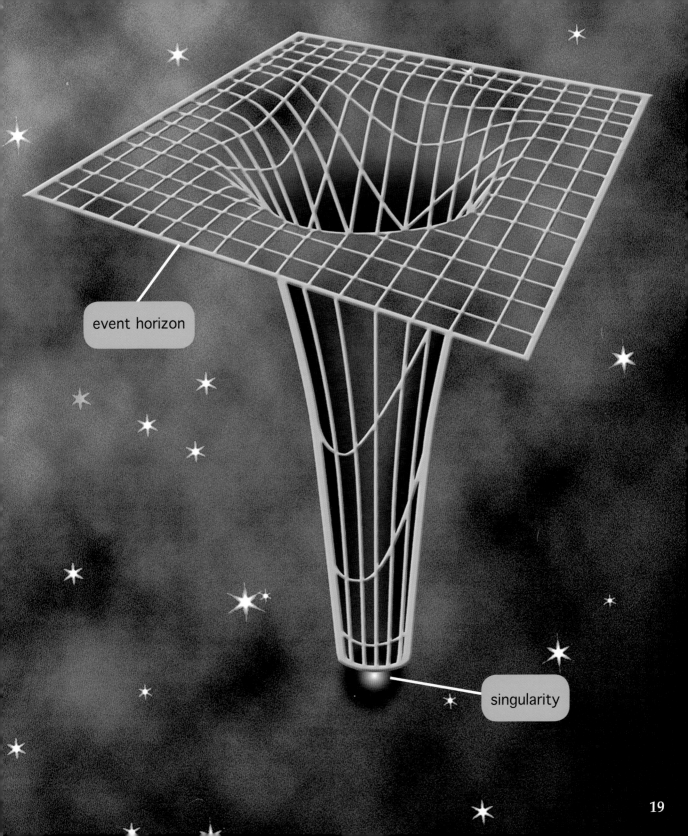

event horizon

singularity

19

Inside a Black Hole

The nearest black hole is about 1,600 light-years away from Earth. And our Sun will never become one. It doesn't have enough mass. So there's no danger of our solar system getting sucked into a black hole.

But scientists have imagined what it would be like if a person did enter a black hole. Once past the event horizon, there would be no turning back. Any light from a flashlight would disappear downward. The person's body would speed up as it fell. The heat would be unbearable. The person's arms, body, and legs would stretch into long strings before being completely pulled apart. In just a matter of seconds, the person would be squashed into a point smaller than an atom.

The same thing happens to all matter in a black hole. It speeds up as it falls. It gets hotter as it's pulled downward. It breaks apart and is squashed into a small point.

FACT: A black hole with the same mass as Earth would fit in your palm.

Gravity inside the black hole pulls on objects, making them long and thin like a rubber band.

Sizes of Black Holes

Astronomers believe black holes form in two sizes. Supernovas create stellar holes. These black holes are usually 10-24 solar masses. Their event horizons are only a few miles across. Stellar holes are the most common type of black hole.

Supermassive holes form at the centers of large galaxies. Scientists think these black holes might be created when galaxies form. These holes can be billions of solar masses in size. Their event horizons can be as large as our solar system.

Every galaxy probably has a supermassive black hole at its center. The center of our galaxy, the Milky Way, is home to a supermassive hole. This black hole may have millions—or even billions—of times more mass than our Sun.

FACT: In our galaxy, one out of every 1,000 stars has enough mass to make a black hole.

an artist's illustration
of a dust ring around a
supermassive black hole

Searching Space

Almost everything astronomers know about outer space comes from studying light. They use telescopes to detect energy such as **X-rays** and radio waves. Astronomers work with **spectroscopes**, cameras, and computers. It takes a lot of math to analyze all the data they gather.

How hard can it be to find an exploding star? It's tougher than you might think. Supernovas only brighten the sky for about six months. Light from galaxies and dust between stars make explosions hard to see. Astronomers take pictures of the sky on different nights. They compare the pictures to find stars that suddenly grow bright.

Astronomers find a few hundred supernovas every year. You probably won't see one close to home. Only a few supernovas occur in our galaxy every 100 years.

X-ray: an invisible high-energy beam of light

spectroscope: an instrument used to study light

This radio telescope, known as the Very Large Array, has allowed scientists to see star births, supernovas, and possibly the black hole at the center of the Milky Way.

an image taken by *Chandra*, showing jets streaming from a supermassive black hole in the Centaurus A galaxy

Finding Invisible Holes

Light cannot escape a black hole. And if an object doesn't emit light, people can't see it. Scientists must look for clues to find these invisible black holes.

One clue scientists look for is light that bends or mysteriously disappears. If a star was falling into a black hole, it's light would bend, as if being pulled downward. Wobbling stars are another clue. If a star tips around like a spinning top, a black hole could be to blame.

Scientists most often study X-rays to find black holes. The matter pulled into a black hole gets extremely hot. When the atoms are millions of degrees, they emit X-rays. Just before the atoms crash into the singularity, the X-rays are pushed into space. The X-rays rush away from the black hole in streams called jets. Spacecraft such as the *Chandra X-ray Observatory* can detect these jets that travel almost as fast as the speed of light.

Extraordinary Space

Deep in space, far beyond our home on Earth, amazing things are happening. Stars are dying, exploding, and forming dense, invisible places. The universe contains billions of black holes. In fact, scientists estimate that a supernova creates a new black hole every second.

Of course, we can't see most of this happening. The universe is just too big for that to be possible. But scientists continue to study what they can see. Who knows what supernovas and black holes can tell us about our galaxy and beyond?

Scientists discovered a supermassive black hole at the center of the Sombrero galaxy in 1990.

Glossary

element (El-uh-muhnt)—a basic substance in chemistry that cannot be split into simpler substances

galaxy (GAL-uhk-see)—a large group of stars and planets

gravity (GRAV-uh-tee)—a force that pulls objects together; gravity increases as the mass of objects increases or as objects get closer

light-year (LITE-yihr)—a unit for measuring distance in space; a light-year is the distance that light travels in one year

molecular cloud (muh-LEK-yuh-lur KLOUD)—a cloud trillions of miles across made mostly of hydrogen atoms bound together; new stars form deep within the cores of molecular clouds

neutron star (NOO-tron STAR)—a dark, spinning star with little mass

solar mass (SOH-lur MASS)—the amount of matter in the Sun; one solar mass is equal to the mass of the Sun

spectroscope (SPEK-tra-skohp)—an instrument used to study light

X-ray (EKS-ray)—an invisible high-energy beam of light

Read More

Baker, David and Heather Kissock. *Probing Space.* Exploring Space. New York: Weigl, 2010.

Gross, Miriam J. *All about Space Missions.* Blast Off! New York: Rosen Pub. Group's PowerKids Press, 2009.

Jefferis, David. *Space Probes: Exploring Beyond Earth.* Exploring Our Solar System. New York: Crabtree Pub., 2009.

Internet Sites

FactHound offers a safe, fun way to find Internet sites related to this book. All of the sites on FactHound have been researched by our staff.

Here's all you do:

Visit *www.facthound.com*

Type in this code: 9781429660044

Super-cool stuff! Check out projects, games and lots more at **www.capstonekids.com**

Index